It happened to A bully picked on me

illustrated by
Adam Blackledge

First published in the UK in 2005
by PANGOLIN BOOKS
Unit 17, Piccadilly Mill, Lower Street,
Stroud, Gloucestershire, GL5 2HT.

Copyright © 2005 Bookwork Ltd.

A CIP catalogue record for this book is
available from the British Library.

ISBN 1-84493-019-X

Printed in the UK by Goodman Baylis Ltd.

GETTING HELP WHEN YOU ARE BEING BULLIED

If you are being bullied, it is important that you tell someone what is happening and talk to them about how you are feeling. Tell your mum or dad, or a teacher at school. You can get help from ChildLine, or the NSPCC. They will not tell anyone about you unless you want them to or you are in danger.

ChildLine
(www.childline.org.uk)
If you have a problem, ring ChildLine on 0800 1111 at any time – day or night. Someone there will try to help you find ways to sort things out.

NSPCC
(www.nspcc.org.uk)
The NSPCC has a helpline on 0808 800 5000 which never closes. There is always someone there to talk to if you are unhappy, worried or scared about something in your life. You can also e-mail them on help@nspcc.org.uk

"I used to have lots of friends at school. There were Azim and Mandy and Jo, and my special friend Alex.

We all sat together in the classroom, and at lunch time we played together outside. School was fun and I was happy. "

Then, one day, a new person came to school. The new person hated me and I didn't understand why.

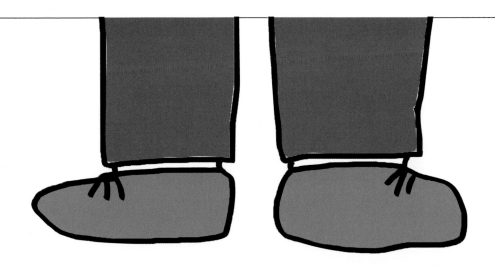

Sometimes it was because
I was wearing lace-up
shoes, and sometimes
it was because my hair
was curly, and sometimes
it was *just because.*"

"I gave the new person a secret name – Newbie. Newbie snatched my toys and hit me when no one was looking. And when I said I'd tell, Newbie called me horrid names, and said I would be sorry if I did.

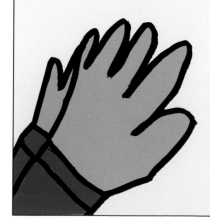

I felt sick a lot. And my tummy ached a lot. Then school was scary and I was unhappy. "

"Mandy and Azim and Jo said
they didn't like me any more.
It was because Newbie told them
not to, but I didn't know why.
Then even my special
friend Alex didn't like me."

"So I sat on my own, and played on my own. Azim and Mandy and Jo and Alex played with Newbie, who hated me. My teacher told me to join in. She didn't know that Newbie hated me and wouldn't let me join in."

"One morning, I told Dad that I was feeling sick. He said I would feel better when I got to school.

But he didn't know
that Newbie had
come to school
and hated me. **"**

"I tried to hold Mum very, very tightly when we got to school, to make her stay with me. I wasn't so scared when she was there. She said I would be alright when I saw my friends.

But she didn't know
that Newbie had
come to school
and hated me. 〞

One morning, I didn't want to get out of bed. Mum asked me if I was unhappy, and I said I was ok.

She asked me why I didn't want to get up and go to school, and I said I didn't know. "

"Every day I cried a lot. I got angry with Mum and Dad and they got cross with me. Everything had changed. One day, I told Mum that I hated my hair and I hated my shoes too. I told Mum I was going to cut off all my hair."

"Then Mum and Dad took me to talk to my teacher. My teacher asked me why I was unhappy. I couldn't speak. My face went red and I didn't know what words to say."

"My teacher asked me
if I was being bullied.
But I didn't know
what that meant
until Dad explained.

And then I cried and
said that I missed my
special friend. I told
my teacher that
Newbie hated me and
I was frightened."

"Mum and Dad and my teacher said I was brave to tell them about Newbie. They said I should have told them before.

But I didn't feel brave.
I felt very small. I felt like
the hamster I once saw
in a pet shop that was
shaking all the time. I felt
like a shaking hamster. "

"Mum and Dad and my teacher say that school will be better now – now I've told them about Newbie. But I'm not sure. How do they know? How can they make Newbie like me instead of hate me?

How can they look after me at school? Dad says I can go to another school if I like, but I don't want to go to a new school. Someone there may hate me too."

"When Newbie snatched my toy last week, I said bravely, 'Give it back.' And Newbie did, and hasn't snatched again. I feel safer now.

Newbie isn't horrid to me any more, but school will never be the same. And Newbie still hates me, I can tell."

"Alex sits with me again and says we can look after each other now. Azim and Mandy and Jo may play with me again soon. Perhaps they will play with me tomorrow."